THREE POEMS

HANNAH SULLIVAN

Three Poems

FABER & FABER

First published in 2018
by Faber & Faber Ltd
Bloomsbury House
74–77 Great Russell Street
London WC1B 3DA

Typeset by Hamish Ironside
Printed in England by Martins the Printers, Berwick-upon-Tweed

A CIP record for this book is available from the British Library

ISBN 978-0-571-33767-5

4 6 8 10 9 7 5 3

Contents

YOU, VERY YOUNG IN NEW YORK

Rosy used to say that New York was a fairground.
'You will know when it's time, when the fair is over.'
But nothing seems to happen. You stand around

On the same street corners, smoking, thin-elbowed,
Looking down avenues in a lime-green dress
With one arm raised, waiting to get older.

Nothing happens. You try without success
The usual prescriptions, the usual assays on innocence:
I love you to the wrong person, *I feel depressed*,

Kissing a girl, *a sharpener*, sea urchin, juice cleanses.
But the senses, laxly fed, are self-replenishing,
Fresh as the first time, so even the eventual

Sameness has a savour for you. Even the sting
When someone flinches at *I love you*
Is not unwelcome, like the ulcer on your tongue

Whetted on the ridges of a tooth.
And when he slams you hard against the frame,
The pore-ticked sallow bruise seems truer

Than the speed, the spasm, with which you came.
So nothing happens. No matter what you try,
The huge lost innocence at which you aimed

Recedes like long perspectives, like the sky
Square at the end of Fifth whitening at dawn
Unseen, as you watch the unlit cabs go by.

~

The White Rose bars opened very early in the morning; I recall waiting in one of them to watch an astronaut go into space, waiting so long that at the moment it actually happened I had my eyes not on the television screen but on a cockroach on the tile floor.

All summer the Park smelled of cloves and it was dying.
Now it is Labor Day and you have been sleeping through a rainstorm,
Half aware of the sewage and frying peanut oil and the ozone
Rising in the morning heat, and the sound of your roommate hooking the chain,
Flipping ice cubes into a brandy balloon, pouring juice over them,
Ruby Sanguinello, till they giggle, popping their skins. The freezer throbs.
He has been beating a man he met on Craigslist, he has been dreaming:
Old New York, a James novel, a Greenwich Village Christmas,
A certain kind of frost in the Meatpacking District, and the smell of the
    carcasses
Dull with the tang of freezing blood beside the skip of the Hudson wind.
You have been thinking of the building opposite at night, the lights
Going off one by one, a diminished Mondrian, one ochre square
Where a woman undresses for the city, stroking her puffy thighs.
You hear him talking on the phone about you, his '*petite innocente*'.
All summer you have been eating peaches from the greenmarket.
Overripe in September they need to rest in the icebox, sitting with their bruises.
All summer you have been dreaming of Fall and its brittle confection of
    branches.

~

Lying awake in the fat pulse of November rain, as the bond market falls
And the art market gets nervous, starts to freeze up, and hipsters
Keep on trying to sell huckleberry jam from Brooklyn and novelists
Keep on going to Starbucks to craft their sagas, adjusting their schemas,
Picking like pigeons at the tail of the morning croissant,

As the bartenders figure out the winter cocktail lists, telling each other
That Cynar, grapefruit bitters, and a small-batch Mezcal will
Be trending in the new year, even though guests are still going to be wanting
Negronis at weddings, gin and tonics on first dates, Manhattans before
Moving upstairs, away from the camera phones, on illicit business . . .

Schramsberg '98 is working well for Caitlin in the nouveau Bellini.
Jed crafts a drink from porter, coffee rum, and Brachetto d'Acqui,
It can only be written in Chinese but is ordered as 'the vice grip',
Its taste is whipped cream and kidneys, beer bitter and honeyed.
He makes it for the girl in leathers with a face like the Virgin Mary.

You are listening to Bowie in bed, thinking about the hollows
Of his eyes, his lunatic little hand jigs, longing for Berlin in the seventies.
You are thinking of masturbating but the vibrator's batteries are low
And the plasticine-pink stick rotates leisurely in your palm,
Casting its space-age glow into the winter shadows.

✍

The splinter in your eye is the best magnifying glass.

Moving in the bathroom at Christmas, plucking your eyebrows, shaving,
(On Friday Trinh will be back and you will take two Advil and lie
On a table in Chelsea holding yourself open, 'stretch it' she says,
Irritably sometimes, and 'stretch' as lavender wax wells

Voluptuously in hidden places, and 'turn' as you kneel on all fours
So she can clean you up behind and, still parting you open, her fingers
Spend one moment too long tissuing off the dead wax with almond oil and
'All done' she pats, producing hot towels); then moving lightly
Over the floor, taking medicines with last night's overnight-out
Brackish water in a coffee mug; taking a levothyroxine, half a Lexapro,
Some vitamins to ward off colds, one to reduce PMS, some other crap
You bought in a basement discount store with a cold, last Monday,
From a man who thought you might be low in magnesium, he said this
While eating vegan candy from a ripped-out pack snatched
From his own counter. Then the weighing, the exhalation on the scales,
A finger callipering for fatness, a finger slipping in to check the cervix –
And walking out of the house into a world overwhelmed with rain and light
    snow,
At more than capacity, so the taxi drivers are only in the middle lane
And the rose sellers have stayed home.

   ❧

The consciousness of the finite, the menaced, the essentially invented state twin-
kles ever, to my perception, in the thousand glassy eyes of these giants of the
mere market.

Evening comes without seeing light again. Between you and a window:
The beige Lego-maze of offices, people whose names you don't know.

You should be addressing inefficiencies in online processes,
Mastering multichannel, getting serious about small business,

You have created a spreadsheet with thirteen tabs,
The manager is giving you hell, ordering sushi, cancelling cabs.

The senior partner calls from Newark, 'Thanks team,' (his thin
Voice purrs, he is sipping something), 'let's make it a win–win.'

But in the morning, brushing his new teeth, looking out into the snow's
Huge act of world-effacement, its lethargy, he knows:

Things are illiquid, freezing up. Light is abortive
On the greyscale Park. It's time to short the fucking market.

In Chennai, meanwhile, a man is waiting for your analysis,
Eating his breakfast of microwaved dal and mini-idlis,

Checking the cricket scores on his computer, reading Thoreau,
Wondering what New York looks like at night, in snow.

He is applying to Columbia, NYU Stern, and Stanford GSB.
He thinks of going abroad as an attempt to live deliberately,

Imagining the well-stacked fires in iron-fenced Victorians,
The senior partner's grace under pressure, his Emersonian

Turn of phrase, the summers spent sailing, the long reaches
Of sand loosely threaded with grass on Cape Cod beaches.

❧

Evening comes without eating anything except a whoopee-pie
You find leftover in the kitchen from someone's birthday surprise.

The malted cream of the filling is so rich it clumps like shit.
You lick it off your fingernails and google the bakery's website.

On Yelp someone has written, 'This case of cakes smells so good
If I ever have to go on a respirator (*knock on wood*)

I hope they use this cake case as my respirator.' Smiling at the screen,
A flicker of dry tongue now, a dopamine prick, as the Ritalin kicks in.

It has something about it of the narrow room silk-lined
With Flemish tapestries you once dreamt about being locked in.

Your psychiatrist said it would help your productivity,
But it feels like drawn-out sex on coke, like something dirty.

The bakery is in Astoria, on Broadway and 28th.
On Street View you look at strangers' faces, at the averted gaze

Of men in sportswear smoking in front of F*MOUS BRANDS,
At takeout bikes, nail salons, Turkish ice-cream stands,

And a grocery store with an unlit sign, 'Hot Coffee',
The slow passing of a cortège in March sleet, the poverty.

Last week *New York* magazine said Queens was getting hip:
At Club 19, 'Manhattan transplants chill and sip

Cold hoppy Krušovice, whisky sours, and Staropramen.'
On Fridays, a pop-up serves tonkotsu miso ramen.

You wonder what it means to define Astoria's 'epicenter',
Or press panini with 'finesse', what the median two-bed rent is.

Once a year you go in a cab to the Bohemian Beer Garden
And eat pink, flayed kielbasa, penile and artery-hardening,

While elderly men dance to a band in blue embroidered hose,
Holding their elbows rigidly, like waxed Pinocchios.

Your friends wear flannel and McDonald's name badges,
They talk about Ben Bernanke and Isabel Marant wedges.

You are slightly disappointed in Obama's domestic policy,
You think the great American novelist is David Foster Wallace.

The epigraph to *The Pale King* is from Frank Bidart,
It is about pre-existing forms and formal questions in art.

CTRL + N is jammed in the spreadsheet of your mind,
Nothing seems real or right, so you just press send.

Then a smear of olive lipstick, and you walk out into the night,
Into the breeze, the smell of roasting, the rich quarters of delight,

And as you are dancing in a suit skirt to the Killers' 'Mr Brightside',
Feeling the anthem soar and rise, he makes the PowerPoint slides;

You will present them in the morning to the client, while he
Sleeps in a fruit and urine breeze beneath a linen sheet.

ॐ

*Forms leaned together in the taxis as they waited, and voices sang, and there
was laughter from unheard jokes, and lighted cigarettes outlined unintelligible
gestures inside.*

Now you are meeting them for Pisco sours at the Peruvian dive bar,
Now plans have changed, it is April, and the first hot day of the year

Has exploded from nowhere. Skin is as profuse and white as funeral flowers.
You are heading downtown, and the cabs are angrier than ever, wasps
Darting between thin panes of glass, and the shape of the traffic
Bulges and breaks in waves while the slam and the slam-*hold* of horns
Sings a scale of human frustration, of the boredom of boxes, as the radio
Dribbles on and off 'Crazy in Love' and you check Facebook on your iPhone:
Kate is photographing durians in Shanghai, Zena was born this morning,
Claire is drying homemade pasta, Elina wishes she could play guitar,
Arlo is flying LHR–SFO, upgraded out of H to J, and your mother asks
To be your friend again, but the request just hangs in the sidebar.

The wind is blowing road-dirt through the window. It catches in your lens.
You are still reading as you move the plastic on the cornea, blinking.
It is still there as you type a happy birthday, pulling your tights down,
And 'The splinter in your eye . . .' thinking, for some reason, about Paris
And the street market on the Rue Mouffetard, wanting to be in Europe,
Remembering your breasts at seventeen and the smell of frying fish
In a cheap hotel, lying while he showered, legs splayed up the wall.
Now he is 'happy Friday!' in Los Feliz drinking gin and you like it.
Three people comment on your update and the driver keeps staring
Dolefully at you in the mirror, long-nosed, surgically examining
Your crotch, a poet of the quick cab change, watching even as you cross
Fifth and the long perspectives open out, into white light, into the infinite.

Here is infinity obscured by a bus, an advert for night classes.
There was infinity and the cab window was gravel-pocked.
Here is infinity again but the driver is outstaring you, unsmilingly
Bent on your feet, the curve of your thighs, still slamming and slam-
Holding the horn as the cab veers east and you see Rosy on the street
Smoking with an older man, the man she is trying to seduce, frail
Despite the biker boots, loosely touching his arm, taking his wrist, waving.
Now you step out of the cab bare-legged into the salty evening,

And a boy model calls out 'ciao bella', and W. H. Auden's house
Is still La Palapa, and you tip him heavily because it is almost summer.

The thing about being very young, as you are, is the permeability
Of one person to another, so when the guys buying sangria say
You should come to Williamsburg you say yes, eat the last orange slice
Skin and all, and do the sideways dive on their laps so the cab takes five.
Rosy strokes your hair absent-mindedly, ignoring the bankers.
Her fingers smell of Camel Lights and lavender, and she is laughing.
'You know his wife left him for a woman.' Her knees are bony.
'We even smoke the same cigarettes.' What do they talk about?
Derrida's late work on gifts, the modalities of power. Last week
In the Bobst stacks they were looking for the same book on Beckett.
'I bent down and I asked him,' she is leaning forwards, whispering
With wine breath in your ear, 'I said I want you to do these things,'
Occluded, a list – the things he might do – you think about her spidery
Cut-out dress, backless, 'but he walked off'. Maybe his hearing is failing.
Maybe he just isn't into her. 'It's not like I want to marry him or anything.'

No one is sure what to say hours later, whipped by the return of winter
Wind on a rooftop in Brooklyn, as she tells the story again,
Lavishly drunk, buoyant, 'Rosy is a beautiful girl and she wants you inside her'.
No one is sure what to say, but it gives one of the bankers an in,
And she is gone, lacing his fingers, leaving her yellow duffel coat.
She is gone so you photograph the view and upload it to Twitter.
She is gone, leaving you alone on a rooftop with a German sculptor,
'Ich arbeite aber lieber mit Holz', *I prefer to work with wood.*
Sometimes the smaller figures are cast in yellow bronze.
Each time she says the word *aesthetic* you suppress laughter.
And then you see him, the man you are hiding from, coming up the stairs,
Alone, in all his specificity: the darting glance fastened elsewhere.

The conceptual installation is in a disused church in Mitte
Not so far from the Hackesche Höfe, 'if you know it?'
He has seen you now and he is here and, as he says your name,
You nod keenly at her, 'the figures are made from locust wood,
With olive wood I was less satisfied', they are painted in mineral colours,
Jade, 'Lapislazuli, is it?' You ask about the sanding tools she uses.
And then to avoid him looking at you, you say all the words for wood
And minerals you know: beryl, emerald, aquamarine, garnet,
Cypress and chestnut, ficus wood, spreading planes, *Kastanie* . . .
When he says 'you've lost weight, you look great' which is true
(He dumped you) you think of elderberry and magnolia, quietly pulling
At the silver-starred skirt, pulling it over the ripple of your thighs.
But when he says one more, for old time's sake, you say why not
And sit rigidly in a cab, crossing the Brooklyn Bridge beside him.

❧

You take your clothes off when he puts his hands over your nipples.
No murmured approbation. His fingers run along the fat, supple
Above the pubic bone, the white flesh below your hips,
Pressing and stroking it like someone testing the grass for a picnic.

Outside the subway train rolls and exhales and the hot water
Comes on as the pipes cough and the air is thick as a basement sauna.
The window cries with droplets, and the long line of Fifth
Is lost behind the IKEA curtains and yet, despite all this,

Despite the sweat, the egg-white liquid stretching between your legs,
The irregular strawberry pattern on his hairless back and pecs,
There is something reserved about it, something classical and staid,
Like a Noh play where a blind man beats a cripple, or like a ballet

Still in rehearsal, the movements unsounded, as the bedframe
Taps percussively and wet skin plucks on skin. It is all the same:
He turns you through positions, expertly restaging old routine,
Until you end up head down, examining the duvet's bobbling,

Trying out the bad banana taste of Durex on your tongue,
Fucked deeper as he eases a finger in, the nail beckoning
Inside the hole, around the clenched twitch of resistance.
It tightens like a toothache. And now you are moving

Faster together, beating out time, until he slams you hard
Into the bedstead and you knock your collarbone. A deep retarded
Wave of pain. Then the surrender as you start to come and squeeze
Against him, while he pulls you backwards, lightly as Thai yoga, easily.

Afterwards you lie in marshy sheets, hearing the subway trains
Increase in frequency, the pipes' morning aubade, the cries
Of women upstairs waking children, looking at water stains
Running across the plaster and the newly painted ceiling rose's

Sad modesty, its oak leaves, touching the moisture on your thighs.
And instead of saying 'I should go', you mouth oak and elm, pine
And juniper. Poplar, tasting your mascara drips. Out loud you say
'I love you', waiting the requisite three beats, wiping away

A clump of old black Maybelline, watching the retraction
Of his toes beneath the sheets, their waisted shape, an action
Familiar as the two black hairs on each. An hour later,
Walking home on Fifth, you are still thinking of them, sated

By self-abjection, stuffing down some pineapple cubes
Bought at a metal hot-dog cart. Your lips feel tight and bruised;

His flesh, the enzymes in the juice. You are looking for a lighter,
Holding your shoes and a fist of dollar bills as it brightens

Quickly into pink flamingo dawn. In winter, night seeped
Gently from the sky, like red wine stains in watery bleach.
Now it is April and another summer. As you go past the subway
An older, also shoeless guy leaps out and shouts, 'Girl, hey'.

He starts to twirl a topless bowler and it dips like an early swallow.
He raps, 'I love *you*, girl', getting low, and the sky over the Park
Whitens in a punched-out square, as one unlit cab follows
Another down Fifth and, through tears, you are laughing.

REPEAT UNTIL TIME

THE HERACLITUS POEM

ποταμοῖσι τοῖσιν αὐτοῖσιν ἐμβαίνουσιν ἕτερα καὶ ἕτερα ὕδατα ἐπιρρεῖ (DK 22, B12)

On those who step into the same rivers, different and different waters keep on flowing . . .

The picked mosquito bites scab over, resin sap.
The bites are as itchy as ever, and the anaesthetic river
Still concentrates its cold, but the ankles are different this summer,
Less lean, veinier, slower in the river.
Other old women step delicately into the same floodwater,
But the river is different without the nesting moorhens,
And magpies hovering by their uncracked eggs.

There is no stepping twice in same or different rivers.
Nor would anyone step once if she hadn't first shivered,
Toes spooning in the mud, watching an older sister
Striding through grasses, imperiously batting off butterflies.

The river cracks, slides on, a parquet floor for hens.
Clouds filter sea, snow hollows flint. March brings new rains.

When things are patternless, their fascination's stronger.
Failed form is hectic with loveliness, and compels us longer.

The horse chestnut gets on tediously with its leaves,
Provides spiked toys, diets middle-aged in winter,
Gets low-carb skeletal, squash lean, only to
Have another go with the old Coolwhip come spring.

The oak tree is absurd as new parents amazed
That a baby's nails need cutting, dead keratin: so slick
So dull, that eternal kernel rigmarole,
The bee-sucked flower, the pig-shat nut,
From which, what junky miracle, new oak trees grow?

The pollarded tree is subtler, its season a fungal autumn.
The branches that were husbanded will never grow clean.
But stunted they stay, an old woman's cobbled knees,
Thick legs beneath a butterball skirt, a green flare,
Her skirts lifted high as she dances to wedding music.

Rolled-up sleeves around each cut-back head
End in slender new sprouts,
Crooked forearms shot from the bark.

You think of Alabama at noon,
A quiet clapboard church,
White shirts rolled up, dust motes
Antsy on the windows, in the heat,
An uncertain hosanna.

It is hard to say if there is progress in history.

1.3

You see them all together and then the aspect alters;
Repetition is inexact, eternal return is falsehood.

1961, a street in Hollywood, a famous photo shoot:
Black cats are trying out to play the title role
In *The Black Cat*, a movie based on Poe, the whole thing flopped . . .

At first, you see the group, the collective noun –
A scattering of beanbags in the sun,
A clutch of black cats straining on their leashes,
And all the plaid mid-calf-length skirts, steam-pressed at dawn,
All the kitten heels and bat-winged Aviators,
Women smiling as if suddenly free in the Reno divorce courts,
Even the thick-ankled turning out their feet,
Nervous as debutantes . . .

Taken together, the cats are alien,
Eerie and luminous as silkscreen Marilyns . . .
But then the interest changes again:
One has a brush of bobcat tail, a milk-foam hairy chin,
A pompom peers out of a zipped-up bag, tip-tongued,
And one throws a winsome look behind himself, apart,
Flashing the squeezed-lime eyes that make a feline movie star.

And a blond kid in a tapestry waistcoat
Watches a big sullen cat on a diamanté leash,
While an older woman in peep-toes throws a hip out,
Squeezing her cat like a tantrum,
Watching him letting his black cat wander wherever.
She knows that 1960 was the future and JFK is in office.
His mother is wondering if she could be pregnant again.
She wears space-age Courrèges like emmenthal.

He is waiting for the sixties to start, for the violence to be real.
He looks like David Bowie on the cover of *Young Americans*,
Uranium-bright hair, a softly permed disco halo.

2.1

Days may be where we live, but mornings are eternity.
They wake us, and every day waking is absurdity;
All the things you just did yesterday to do over again, eternally.

The clench of tonsil on extra tonsil is an oyster only once,
Once, the blood and itch of broken skin, and afterwards indifference,
The boredom of the weeping aromatic bedsores only once.

But, forever fumbling for the snooze button, the gym is there
Forever, and the teeth silt over yellow to be flossed, and there
Will be, in eternity, coffee to be brewed and that moment in the shower
When you open your mouth and rhotacise the water and just stand there,
Stupid bliss of hot water, tongue-tingling, steaming the shower.

2.2

Yes, the hipsters crumble their kouign-amann in San Francisco,
Fog lifts away like garage doors, MacBooks get going.
A girl with drug sores rocks by a steamed-up Bikram studio.

Women pour milk on Kashi for the men from Tinder in the Mission,
Wondering if they didn't come because of the Last Words or the sertraline.
Or maybe it is just what happens when you get older or heartbroken.

And the flamers in the Castro from last night order oat pancakes,
Bacon crisp in a cross, white lozenge of butter, dispelling headaches,
While the pastry chef folds cinnamon into tres leches cakes.

Su-Yen pauses lordly before he crosses, reproving his owner
With a shake of his standard-size poodle head at each corner,
His jaw primitive and cautious (*cave*!) as the mosaic dog in Pompeii.

And you ease out behind huge Ray-Bans, counting the avenues
Of rubbery ficus trees, past ox-tongue taquerias,
Into the tangle of collapsible concrete freeways.

Grey coaches carry hooded children south to the Valley,
A coder who grew up in a car in Hawaii is drinking a Snapple,
A quant checks the calories on a granola puck and checks Facebook.

So no one sees the sparrowhawk stall in the outside lane.
And he is himself surprised by the deer in the windscreen,
The plump bunny rump, the hooves in child's pose. Balasana.

It took the car out in the early hours. On the seat
The bored drool of its jaw, the crushed pearlescent teeth
Turned to the side, like someone whimpering at sleep.

2.3

7 p.m.: commuting home: arrest.
Trader Joe's, the Daly City multiplex.
Repetition's sense of comedy
Unsheathed as architectural poverty:
Beige curves on Taco Bells,
And fog, the old dry ice machine.

Three sooty wraiths
Fade on the bridge like figures on a vase,
Faded already in an eighteenth-century house –
Stooped, waterthinned
Chinoiserie.

Some kid from Stanford GSB
Enters the 101 the wrong way round.
He kills two Puerto Rican passengers
And the taxi driver.
DUI. The Dean writes: 'Our community
Can only get stronger
From this manifest tragedy.'

An Audi TT in the next lane gets rammed:
The driver pops a nicotine gum,
Even though he is already chewing one:
Sweet watermelon shell in gum strings.
His wife goes through to voicemail.
Parked up, his face mashes into the wheel.

It is July and the fog falls
Like a solid,
Like raisins in soda at elBulli.
The world tastes of molecules,
Palpitates in ozone.

2.4

True form is often seen only in retrospect, too late.
Sometimes streams peter out; sometimes a grand Niagara lies in wait.

On August 5, 1914, Henry James was at home at Rye,
Wearing a watch-chain, thinking about being British,
Writing to Howard Sturgis: 'The taper went out last night . . .
The plunge of civilization into this amiss, this abyss
Of blood and darkness . . .' Theodora Bosanquet,
His secretary, takes down dictation, hearing the master
Becoming orotund to the click of the Remington keys.

That year it was the finest of English summers.
In the fields outside, the farmer's boy
Rolls up bright bales, Valkyrie braids, of hay.
Drought beats older gold of them beneath a sky
That stays itself until November, and sparrows
Take their perches on the drying hay, waiting,
Listening for something to happen overseas.
'A nightmare of the deepest dye . . .'
And yet the Channel is as 'blue as *paint*',
Neat as the rim on a soup plate from Delft,
Opaque, tin-glazed, and bold as the horizon
On medieval maps, a clumsy brushwork line
Drawn to disguise the fear of what is limitless.

'The nearness of the horrors in perpetration just beyond.'

At night, James sees the farmer's boy die, alone, over and over.
In the morning, the insect-filled heady magnificence of Indian summer.

3.1

True form is overlaid, like moss on broken tiles.
But scoured and weeded back, a mosaic face peers out and smiles.

The face in the toilet mirror could be anyone,
Lips tacky with the lint of two small Cabernets.
And then the seatbelt sign goes on and you stagger back,
As the undercarriage hauls itself, hauls itself down,
The local time is coming up to seven.
You are in a holding pattern over Heathrow.

In Greenford, Northolt, the places you were little in,
Curtains are being drawn in pre-war terraces,
Cornflakes are shaken out like leaves.
There is the anachronism of milkmen.
Only one house is un-insulated, red-roofed.
Your fingers grip the passport's brown chamois.

Someone who has been abroad can never come home again:
London is home and it is foreign.

Today there is no hurry, because you have no luggage.
And there is no one to meet you in arrivals,
There is only the emptiness of the Terminal 5 cathedral lighting,
The pop of a Krispy Kreme sign and the tan embonpoint
Of Scotch bottles after customs to caress: the last way
After travelling so long to delay returning.

Home: a queue of open-toed sandals by the door,
The Velcro straps slack, guileless as dogs' tongues,
The Persil-white brocade of laundered sheets,
And on the wall the Harvard calendar you bought them,
The knife-smoothed fondant of the frozen Charles,
Only your name against the day of coming home.

And then it is 10 a.m., and the stairs creak, corseted,
As the grizzled dog runs epileptic with joy into the hall,
And your father's hand whitens on the banister
As he eases himself down, tanned like a skier,
His eyes turning inward, puzzled, the pupils contracted,
Your nose finding the blue pile of his dressing gown.

Later you stand in the garage, holding a plastic pony.
There is the long glissando of a motorbike on the arterial road,
A boomerang, the case of Saint-Emilion he didn't get to drink,
The label working loose, the wine maderised,
The Magic Faraway Tree boxed up for grandchildren,
And, in your hand, the flawless yellow hide.

At night you leaf through Blyton in bed,
Crumble the book's spine.
The wine you pour down the outside drain.

Black spars, sediment:
A shipwreck in a bottle.
Clots on the lung.

3.2

There is saying the same thing again in a different form,
There is saying something new in the same form,
There is saying the same thing again in the same form,
There is not much saying something new in a new form.

Coughing in fog, sweet skunk of Jack Herer . . .
An old man lumbering with a mutt, plum-eyed,
Waving his glasspiece at you: *You take pride*
In fucking up the things we fought them for?
His breath is feline, fish-tin in the air,
And yet his choice of hat is not absurd;
The Tenderloin is also gentrified,
Straw Panamas are what the hipsters wear.

Mid-century has never been more chic:
Techies in vintage Levis get a fix
From looking for authentic Mission dives.
I'd like something with egg white and Mezcal.
Angel investors underwrite it all;
The shit-stained can, the iPhone afterlives.

'Golden girls and lads all must,
As chimney sweepers, come to dust.'

Hugh Kenner believed in reasonable rhymes,
Poets as scientists, discoverers of verities:
Must/dust, shade/glade, thought/nought.
In Warwickshire he saw an old man blowing a golden lad.
'We call them chimney sweepers when they go to seed.'

Dandelions go blowsy and grey, get dandruff,
The clean brush is matted with cobwebs.
Children read the hours on dying flowers.

Some words have also lost their pairs:
Some rhymes are only painful memories,
Recycled like family sagas at Christmas, clichés.
The almost-instincts of minor poets.
Below, for example, rhyme's artefacts:

'All days are nights to see till I see thee,
And nights bright days when dreams do show thee me.'

'If this be error and upon me proved,
I never writ, nor no man ever loved.'

What will survive of us?
Larkin thought the answer might be 'love',
But couldn't prove it.

'The drafts folder was the most interesting place.'
'It was always you, in the end.'
'He tried to tell you in his own way.'

Short chains of carbon in the dust,
This is the practical answer.
Old laptops, pacemakers, leg pins.
DNA fibres revealing death's cause.
Emails we sent and drafts we didn't send.
The things we said and those we should've.

Downloaded porn videos reveal
Proclivities that shock our friends:
Cotton gags, string cutting into the clefts
Of twenty-something Japanese schoolgirls.
But nothing filthy enough to interest strangers.

Old lovers cross their legs, refold the paper,
Study the afterimage in the metro window.
No one remembers everything about someone.

A quick armpit wash at 6, a fluster of perfume,
Dancing into tights, two daubs of blood.
A finger pulls vagrant hairs, snags the elastic.
Snow in the second week of December.

But how was it that you smelled afterwards,
On my hands?

3.32

Another dubious rhyming poet: Shelley.
He might, I suppose, have been speaking Platonically,

About 'true love' as intellectual knowledge,
But the jealous Mary thought that it was bilge.

'The heart that loves, the brain that contemplates . . .
One object, and one form,' is dull, he states.

In 1820, he was in love with a girl locked up in a convent,
Two women had killed themselves for him,

Both of his marriages had failed,
He was about to die. He was cruel. He railed:

'True Love in this differs from gold and clay
That to divide is not to take away.'

What crap. E. M. Forster hadn't even come out
When he used it as an epigraph: 'fine poetry',

Says his lame hero, grandly, brooding on sex.
'I never was attached to that great sect . . .' etc.

But later even Rickie finds the *Epipsychidion*
Evasive in its advocacy of free love, 'a little inhuman'.

After all, 'I love you both' is easier to say than hear.
Demolition, a swung weight, it unbalances the ear.

True love yearns always for reciprocation.
So in the end we sit, desolately, at the station,

Waiting with an awkward bunch of lilies for the train,
Watching the one we love walk arm-in-arm into the rain,

Head tilted to one side, laughing as they have always done,
A hand in someone else's hand. Yes, loving more than one . . .

Means multiplying detail, and then its loveliness is gone.
So it means nothing suddenly. You could be anyone.

Nor is the way he curls his feet beneath your feet,
Nor a shabby patch of brown chest hair important, discrete.

No, and the slick wet ostrich feather between your legs,
Is not important as *yours*, but because it connotes sex.

And the turn of his face away, a babyish hiss in orgasm,
Is not something shared, but the key turn of solipsism,

No, none of those things that meant so much survive,
Untarnished, hearing the same things multiplied.

4.1

Cyclical theories of the universe are out of fashion.
But the Big Bang gives you vertigo.
You would take thalidomide, anything!

'Picture it as a partially inflated balloon.'

You think of something red in the Christmas tree,
How it inflates into long-bellied reindeer.
Then, overfilled, they deform, bleach.
How Santa staggers wasted to his sled.
But there is nowhere to be looking from.
The balloon is the whole universe,
So how can you be holding its neck,
Tromboning the rubber band?

And the smell of pine needles
And warmed-through rubber?

'The smoothness and flatness of the universe
Is hard to explain with inflationary models.'
There is the problem of dark energy.

But to think of it all happening over and over,
Universe after universe, each universe flat,
Consumed by fire, then cooling slowly,
Like ice cubes on August afternoons,
Shells and pools, raw eggs whenever checked on,

Only for the freezer to be ravaged by fire
On a hidden fifth dimension
Until a new universe is born?

What, would another bubble form to pop – just so?
Would it be no-pulp OJ next time, too?

4.2

To begin with, everything was nothing
And there was nothing to speak of and no begin with.

No, there was nothing to speak of, before there was everything.
Then (when?) all speed of light and speed of forever, balls of gas,
Bright stars falling into the suck of black holes, radiant plates,
The outward transfer of angular momentum,
Then gas accreting into galaxies, becoming a little more clustered,
Becoming worlds, becoming worlds on which something so comical,
So precise, so utterly *different* from the world, so lovely
As that language of ours, these words, could arise in one of them.

To speak of when and then and moments is a figure of language,
It is language addressing itself to what is not, and to what it is itself not.
Language with its simple action words, verbs:
Ich mag es nicht, vas-y toi, non sum qualis eram,
Language with its 'past' and 'future' and 'present',
Pointing to what it doesn't know, I love you, now, babbling of unicorns.

4.3

Tears and liver spots on the back of the hand,
The comfort again and again of writing something fictional down.

All cancers were once benign,
Then the DNA forgets its prosody
And cells divide interminably:
The raddled beauty of doggerel.

Stained under a microscope,
An ovary is Venice at sunset,
'Too beautiful to be painted' said Monet.
Midas-touched sperm, bulging and fanning.

4·4

July 16, 1945: lightning zigzags, delays.
It is minus twenty minutes, minus nineteen,
It is the world's first countdown.

And if only time could dilate
If only time could dilate *or* speed up
It would be never or it would be game over.
'I never realised seconds could be so long.'
Men push their cheeks together on the lino,
Clench back sneezes. Black boots pinch corns.
And now it is NOW and his knuckles blanch on the post.

$T = 0 = 5:29:45$ a.m.
It is very important that the thunder comes.

But there is so much light, light, heat on the neck.
Feynman discards the welder's glass,
His eye socket ground blind.
The rest see a scatter of antelope arrows,
And a mile-wide aniseed ball, air-sucked orange.
And let there be mountains in the desert.
A half-drawn cartoon bubble waits for the joke,
A red-hot elephant dances on its trunk.
Whose is this wig that blazes from behind?

Light is a scalpel excavating retinas,
A needle caught on an LP, boring into bodies.
And then light turns into sound, into ordinary thunder.
The sound catches up with the light, and the desert howls.

Now nothing will ever be the same again.
And everything will be as it always was.

He ought to say that the Atomic Age has begun.
He feels like a boy who has aced a math test,
The placid pleasure of being specially intelligent,
But to come to the front of the stage, like prize day?
His ribs itch with eczema, sweat in loose tweeds.

Historic moments are as tiresome as first nights,
All lines to fluff, after being cooped up,
The meaning eroded by gabbling in rehearsal.

He is remembering snow in Harvard Yard,
The death of light early and grit-stained slush.
'Afterwards, I remember, the boatman called to us.'
(The words won't come, he fumbles for them.)
Later, 'I am become Shiva, death, the shatterer of worlds.'

Out loud he says, 'It worked.' No glitches.
The Director takes hot thumbs from his belt loops,
And struts across the room. Blood in bruised ears.
'Now we're all motherfucking sons of bitches.'

[And repeat.]

THE SANDPIT AFTER RAIN

Think of a hospital ward at night:
The phone squirming on someone's bedside table,
The doctors descending like robbers on the bed,
The youngest running from a dream he had just begun . . .

1. Stuffing a Chicken

At the start of the journey, before boarding even begins,
Whortleberry tears, brighter than the eyes of swallows,
Smoother than the eggs of moorhens . . .

Things happened in the wrong order, out of nature.
There was that larval froth in the morning in the garden,
Bubbles of spit on the black rosemary sticks,
And in the afternoon the forelocks of a crocus.
At night I took long baths in the penumbra of the streetlight.
And when we saw the foetus on the screen he did not dive,
He was no longer dangling on his cord,
His mouth was no longer snapping like Pac-Man's.
He had filled his womb. Only one baleful eye
Opened in the gloom, closed in the ebbing waters.

This was a week past due. Nothing was favourable.
The neck of the womb was hard and closed.
The midwife couldn't reach to strip the waters.

Try pineapple. Try reflexology in Kilburn.
Or (scanning my notes, I am 35, it might be IVF)
'Try what got you that way, why don't you?'

✍

I try reflexology in Kilburn, acupuncture in Fulham,
Swimming, acupressure, a whole pineapple from Ghana,
More acupuncture. Acupuncture with electric needles,
I get a discount on the final session,
'It wasn't going to work, as I said . . .'
The date must be wrong, miscalculated.
Soon it will be the year of the sheep.
And what was I thinking, moving house?
These things are no good in pregnancy:
Wind, scissors in the bed, moving furniture in vacant spaces,
All these superstitions . . .
Funerals, sitting with a corpse . . .
Eating crab, touching the bride at a wedding . . .

On the front page of the paper,
'C-section surge in China as zodiac sign moves'.
Only one sheep in ten has a chance at happiness.

I lurch along the street
On slippered size 9 piano feet,
The woman who has done everything
She shouldn't do,
Everything unmotherly and queer,
Taboo,
Frantically googling:

taboo pregnancy what not to do
+ dietary restrictions
+ death
+ new year 2015 date

The ice is now abundant
And should be brought into the ice-houses.

The sacrificial victim is prized for its kidneys;
The magpie begins to build.

Hens hatch.
The sun has been through all his mansions.

The last month of winter is time's fullness.
Let me mummify.

☙

Now I wish I had done prenatal yoga and opened my hips.
In San Francisco, I did yoga: it was the month of the breath.
But I never wanted to dedicate my practice to Ganesh,
Or join in the Sanskrit chanting, or be made manifest,
Or only as a size 4 with toned legs.

Om Sahana.
Om Shanti.
What faith did I have in the wisdom of the east?
In hypnobirthing?

I remembered the itchy feeling of lying on a futon,
Masked, while a man who had eaten garlic prawns
Wafted tuning forks, occasionally checking his phone,
Unblocking each stagnant meridian of my soul.
I knew the sob through the plywood wall.
I was afraid of the sadness of energy workers.

I was afraid of meditating,
The damp slug trail, the dangling bit of cotton
Hanging from the shirt, the movements of mouths:
Om . . .
The engineer glossy with concentration
Composing his lips like a bridesmaid in a hotel bathroom,
Om, he blots, the stripes of Revlon Cherry Snow.
The girl who corks her mouth like yesterday's prosecco,
The girl with a neck like a trombone,
Om . . .
The teacher rustling the elaborate sinews of her arms,
But swift and modest as a nun at weekday Eucharist
As she slips a tongue beneath the sound and the sound
Dissolves on the tongue and the stop is gone, *Om* . . .
And there is only this tinny singing,
This wavering *Om* on the stave.

Remember the wedding on Cape Cod, and the sand flies,
And the lobster rolls with mayonnaise made with egg yolks,
Remember the pink champagne and the welts of horseflies?
Atone.

Remember the bad feng shui of the house you sold.
The cross street that fell straight out of the front door,
Past the juice shop with its bags of fibrous pulp
(Clean turmeric, rainbow chard, lace-eaten kale)
Up to the Eichler homes banked with six o'clock fog,
The pert mid-century rooflines?
Atone.

Remember the dated features the stager ripped out,
The blue jay your neighbour said was her mother,
And the levity in the eyes of men who had known death
Everywhere, but found themselves still living,
Putting on weight, joining Facebook,
Picking through the buggies in Noe Valley,
Buying cut lilies and plumcots at the market.
Remember the pink Edwardian chandelier,
And shifting boxes in the cellar of an untenanted house.
Remember the pregnancy you wronged.
Atone for Dolores Street.

Remember the way your nails felt on the doctor's shoulder,
The hissing threat to litigate,
The ill luck you cast into the brown pool of his eye,
In the room with the water cooler and solitaire,
The room for grief, with *Country Life* magazine
And beige mugs scurrilous with rings from half-drunk tea.
Atone with what you have.

🪶

And the day comes when it is time to visit the living,
When the garden was long with gooseberries
And lightning cracked the teacup of the sky.
I remember a honeycomb fence, and thunder,
And running in because we had heard about nuclear rain,
I remember a sofa with ribbed velveteen buttons,
And a blue Burmese kitten charmed down from the fence.
And snow on the telly – that static sound . . .
And standing at the door, waiting for the parquet floor
To tessellate itself, to be whirled weightless.

I remember when time was a ship's container, with luggage
And wine and bananas lashed down to the emptiness.
I remember my father stuffing a chicken for lunch.

2. Hospital Windowsills

why
he lay with his hands like that
not looking at the video clip
or listening to the slop of your heartbeat,
or seeing the embryo's unfinished limbs,
why he was dialysed, drained, pumped with albumin;
why he didn't watch the television you paid for

how
it feels to staunch a neck with your thumb,
poking the gristle back in, how tricky it is;
how small hospital gloves are

if
he waited all night for the cornflakes and ice cubes
or had pleasure in anything

how the foetus lolls in the womb
swelling like a wine cork left out on the counter
dozing, growing its head hair . . .
how hospital car parks look at dawn,
how tiring pregnancy would be,
how you spent his last morning
not visiting, wandering between cafes,
looking for eggs fried not poached;
how he wasn't himself

why the new waxwork lolls in the bed,
the colour of A4 rubbed with Nescafé,
the distressed colour of fake parchment;
blank, dismayed, the worn-off face
of a cloth doll a girl is bored by

that there is no necessary season for things
and birth and death happen on adjacent wards,
that both are labour, halting and starting;
that women are always the middlemen
finding the coins . . .

ave, morituri te salutant.
respice . . .

❧

I felt I was being very brave, once the cramps started.
I tried to let my husband get his sleep.
I lay watching the streetlight through the shutters,
Finding nothing in the sky to listen to.
Even the air ambulance was still,
Squatting like a locust on the roundabout,
And the planes had not begun circling Heathrow:
They were still serving breakfast over Ireland,
Or spiralling like campfires from Treviso.
I thought of their shadows over the Alps;
I wanted to think of snow sifted on snow,
But I kept seeing sharp kneecaps of ice,
And loose pastures of gentians.

And then I was dreaming of a Red Cross plane.
My father was driving us through the chalk cut,
'Look', he said,
And the plane sang into the escarpment
Waggling where the red kites used to fly,
Pluck.
And then there were others, like pub darts,
Pluck. Pluck.

As soon as it was light, the cramps had gone,
And the baby was hiccoughing and the shower was on.
So I lurched downstairs for another bowl of pineapple.
I had finished the raspberry-leaf tea.

Outside the magnolia was getting rheumatism,
It tapped its swollen fingers on the fence.

Spring. Spring.
A little wren on the grass,
Pigeons stacking like Tupperware.

Think of the saltwater eel in the suburban restaurant.
It wants to be rid of the tank, the shriek of lobsters,
The monotonous view of leatherette banquettes,
The off-duty industry folk, greedily appraising,
'Let's do it half sashimi-style, half dry-fried-spicy',
And also not to be rid of the tank, to remain forever
Chosen and not yet chosen, neither living nor dead,
Eddying between two walls of bubbling glass.
Learn something about indifference.

Think of the QE2, the hospital built like a ship,
With views of the waterworks of Edgbaston
And the tall dilapidated red-brick folly
That Perrott built – twin towers
To see his dead wife's grave
Or spy the living woman
Bustling self-satisfied from another's man's hands,
Or both . . .

Think of your father explaining it, ·
How Tolkien twinned the towers in his mind,
Walking from his aunt's house past the gasworks,
Through elm trees, elm trees whispering,
Thinking and not thinking of his mother dying,
Tapping on his teeth the Greek reduplicated perfect.

Think of the wizened nectarines on the windowsill
Like shepherdesses on a mantelpiece.

Think of the windowsill without the nectarines.

Here is the sound dying, and the ragged inhalation,
Here is the open vowel and the stop, *om*.
And here is the shriek at dawn from the other room,
The toddler's quick crescendo of wanting.

Om, om.
His mouth is like a mussel prising open.
Here is the milk. *Mamma.*
Here is the salt you wanted on your tongue.

And then there is the broken shell with its frills and ribs,
The castanet bits in your palm.
In each calcified stripe of white,
A year in which something was living.

Om.

❧

I lowered myself in my blue gown,
I submitted to being shaved. I had sent my last emails.
I felt mulish, like someone who has tidied too many drawers,
Aggrieved with myself and the world.
I was growing still larger, despite the two extra weeks,
And three sweeps, the midwife finicky,
And the foetus unmovable, indifferent.
I had, of course, begun to resent it,
And the insistence on it coming out.

So, surgery. But it was not an emergency.
It wasn't even like cancer. It was more like adenoids.
The surgeon seemed too young,
The anaesthetist had something of the hockey team about her.
There was a cannula and they poked my legs.
It was as if I had been planning to fly to Greece,
But ended up on a coach, listening to the toilet's slurry,
With only a third of a book left,
And a flat warm bottle of San Pellegrino.

I tried to close my eyes, to surrender to time's mechanism,
And then I petrified: feet, knees, thighs, and further up
My hands pawing at nothing, my lungs

Crushed by the bump I felt nothing moving in.
It was like dying at the hairdresser's, fingers
Fluttering soap in the grooves of your ears,
Exchanging pleasantries, *in extremis*.

The anaesthetist worked up my legs,
Tap, tap, swishing her braid: can you feel here?
Here?
I wanted to vomit but my body had no rotation, so I said,
'I want to die', quite loudly, and everyone was angry.
You're not going to die, you're going to have a baby.

Apothanein thelo, I am going to have a baby.
Afterwards we agreed I had not been very brave.

Under a tangle of capillaries,
A baby is dreaming of his old home.
The Sunday morning swimming pool
Of far-off children.

Then yellow glows in the curtains
And his mouth snapdragons open.
The unused breast is filled with pebbles,
The mouth finds its fish lips.

This is the world:
The street-cleaning machine
The slow lob of rubbish
And the binmen calling.

3. When the Egg Meets the Whisk

If you do not weep now, you may never weep.
Because when you return, there will only be a cubicle,
And the nectarines on the hospital windowsill.

Things slump, dirty themselves, become compound.
Mould forms its spores on bread, and sheep get shaggier.
Cherry blossom settles on cars like sunroofs.
Jumpers bobble.

You know all this:
The look of meat minced or raw or browning in the pan,
The newborn baby's eye like a poster of the Aegean,
And how the iris tans, brindles, picks up its sun-spots,
Spins colour like roulette.
And yet you always forget . . .
Like the sand from Petra, when the jar flies from the shelf,
Forgetting its layers . . .

⁏

Think of a children's sandpit after rain,
Seaweed of twigs, blown Costa cups, a capsized sock,
The filthy abandoned homes of snails,

A spade. And beyond the sand, the municipal grass,
With its round fox turds and burrowed loose earth and pellets,
And the hairy scallion clumps that follow bluebells.

Think of the discretion of a bluebell;
Think of municipal grass.

Think of your back at twenty: a map of nothing, a Pacific.
And then the colonies of pain, the trigger points,
The knotty sheaths of fascia you pay people to pound,
The Balkanisation of the muscle groups . . .

Think of the reality of breastfeeding:
Your fingers gleaming like crab-claws under the tap,
The breast pump drying on its rack, the lip valve missing,
The full bottle tipping voluptuously into the carpet pile,
The freezer with its little packs of frozen pastry,
The baby alone in his basket, watching the shadows.
And think of the pop, like champagne, the first time you opened formula –
The magnum bottle, the baby sick as a wedding guest,
And then soft-pillowed with his dummy on your breast.

Think how suffering is, unanimated,
The iron filings of the laughter lines unmagnetised,
Blending with the bruises:
What Crayola, what an Ash Wednesday for a face!

Think of your father's leather valet case,
The navy dressing gown you used to put your nose in.
You hadn't seen them since childhood,
And there they were by the side of the bed, to take home,

The leather with its evenly polished grain,
The dressing gown mended on the shoulder.

Think of a children's sandpit after rain.

❦

This is the world and the entropy of things,
The plugged dyke and the sea coming in,
The emendation and the introduced error,
The floor before a toddler's pasta dinner,
The smooth pool waiting for the novice diver,
The girl's outfit for tomorrow and her mother's,
The first *I love you* and the others.

❦

So we remember the courage of street cleaners,
Because of the hopelessness of their work,
And house painters in seaside towns,
And the charity of shift workers in hospital car parks,
Because they sit drinking tea and smoking,
And do not care for fining the dying.
And the bonhomie of Manhattan psychics,
Squatting in their basements lit like brothels,
When the season refuses to turn,
And women spend Thanksgiving alone.
Everything is dry and dead and unclean,
And love spits for information.

So we remember our own teenage selves,
And their afterlives, and the soft nectarines
We didn't want to buy, and why:

Because of the army veterans in the lift,
And morning sickness tight under the ribs
Like someone trying on a vintage skirt;
Because of the boy in open-wove khaki
With a face like a dollar-store Halloween mask,
Who mobilised the muscles of his chin, the sinews of his neck,
To approximate a smile – to be kind to us.

As we remember our own good enough mother,
Because she was anxious about doing things wrong,
And did things wrong, and loved us.
Because she sang of buses, out of tune.

🌿

Once they began, I was calmer,
I enjoyed the gush of the knife, and the sound of the scissors,
The slop of my bowel being set to one side,
The look on the surgeon's face, his attentiveness and shock,
'Can someone pass me the forceps please?'
And then almost too soon, he was looking away
At the ascension of the 'enormous baby boy',
Rising over the curtain, into the neon ceiling.
And the glowing plinth of green, twitching,
Hacked about . . .

The fish thrashing on the hook that happened to it.
Well, of course: who wants to be born?

And to be hauled out, in a windowless room
Somewhere near Paddington to Radio 5 Live?

To be born purple, your hair scrambled like eggs?
I have never heard a person so incredulous with rage.

And then they couldn't stop the bleeding.
Everything was larger than they thought, they said.
The baby, the placenta, the vessels, even the womb.
So I lay on the table, haemorrhaging,
And the alarm bell rang and the consultant asked
'What uterine tonics have been administered?'
'Oxytocin, ergometrine . . .'

It sounded like a restaurant kitchen.
Someone was washing up the fish knives,
And my husband had a face in his hands,
Grave despite the monkey hat,
Benignant, black-eyed, magnanimous.

꧂

Late on summer Saturdays,
This is what the verger sweeps:
Ombre moons, pistachios, ash,
Hearts cut from upcycled maps,
Scalloped bits of Austen novels,
Hot pushed handfuls of white petals.

This is what the broom releases:
Acetate of Camel Lights,
Pheromones of human fear,
Public libraries' unwashed armpits,
Sweet sweat like a pound cake rising,
Modern roses' nothingness.

This is how things mix together,
Matter's endgame of fawn-dun,
The inevitable greyish
Persil makes its money from.

So when something singular
Comes along, it is a miracle:
Hail tap-dances down the tarmac,
Skittering in its silver shoes.

&

The baby did not look like my father at all,
But there was a resemblance:
Our slight awkwardness with each other.

Neither of us was at our best, that first night –
There was the puff of the pump compressing my legs,
I was giddy from the intravenous morphine, my catheter wept,
And I was amazed – after watching so much arid dialysis –
By the heavy saddlebags of urine beside the bed.
And then there was our mutual Englishness.
We tried to ignore the UV lighting coming under the curtain,
And the hissing mother of the jaundiced twins.

I couldn't reach the plastic crib,
So you lay, all nine and a half solid pounds, in my arms,
And we were both shyly pleased with each other,
A little snobbish with relief and recognition.
That it should be you, after all –
The voice you already knew, the limbs I had already felt.

Weep at the start of the journey, before boarding even begins,
Weep whortleberry tears, brighter than the eyes of swallows,
Deeper than ponds on your father's clean yard,

If you do not weep now, you may never weep.
Because when you return, there will only be a cubicle,
And the nectarines on the hospital windowsill,

So weeping would be for a penumbra of sentiment:
The itch of a lost quotation in a book you cannot find.

4. The Year of Getting Cards

Look at the mantelpiece with its tents.
My life is at a distance from my life
Like the *Telegraph* announcements column,
Not always as interesting as the weather, and certainly
Lacking the true frisson of pleasure
That the elderly take in the dying,
The jilted in the newly engaged.

Look at my breasts, they are school bells,
And there is that pins-and-needles moment
As the ugly distended nipple fills the flange
And then the pulling pulse of the first skimmed milk,
The huge relief of the sea as it reaches the beach
And sprays, and sprays,
Before the sotto voce of the filling bottle,
Cream falling quietly into milk.

It has been the year of life events.
All these things to get a card for.
So I make milk.

I have taken down the cards that were there before.
But they, like these, were full of the feelings I ought to be feeling,
So many Duchamp readymades of grief, so many white toilet fountains,

As these are so many readymades of joy, with bears on,
Capri to Cambridge blue and celadon.

❦

Whether
They were deprived of life
Or died, like molluscs, in their own houses.

Whether
We knew them as president
Or only visit the mansions their descendants resent:
The vestibules smeared with lemon chiffon stone from Caen,
The huddle of cottages against the wind at Hyannisport,
One sealed as it was, strewn with waste paper.

Whether
They die so suddenly everyone stops
And takes the measure of their own lives,
Or slowly in the spread body of an old man.
The dead are all the same.

(I saw Teddy once in a plastic bib:
He was siphoning the meat from a lobster claw.
His light eyes ransacked the ocean.)

The dead recede, beatified,
Like the older mother nursing a baby
Suddenly radiant, *au quatorzième* . . .
Even with that slewed tattoo,
A pale green mermaid powdery with hair . . .

Calls are cancelled on both sides,
Intimacy ossifies
And promises go unfulfilled.
'It will be the making of her',
My father said, behind the curtain.
I was 35, pressed to his words
Like the girl in yellow flannelette,
Poised behind the banisters.

Dull as any family business
Dying is what the dead pass on.

≈

The blur of oxytocin after labour is called joy,
But it is only like the morphine someone dying dies enjoying,
And everyone else is vaguely embarrassed by:
By the way the person dying is enjoying it at last,
By the giggling spew of the bowel in the bed,
And the slightly peremptory wave of the hand, and finally
The long carnival of the final breath,
The body heaving what was inside into the open,
The yellow urine skittling to the floor,
The blood, the sangria rushing through the teeth,
And the maracas in the chest, the maracas, the castanets,
As we sit, little wimpled Puritans with our tissues at the sickbed,
Willing it all to end, an iron lung clamping down on the eccentric oars
    of the ribs,
Wishing them still, wishing for silence, wishing this life lost,
Wishing for it to be odourless, man's loss of the last animal lust.

Yes, let it be odourless.
Just as at birth the placenta is binned and the alien green cord
Is mangled with scissors
By the husband who is holding his breath.

❧

The rich have ponds and lime-green parakeets,
Their brownstone Gothic, their Manhattan views,
And, for company, those who choked in war
Or evening dress, stampeding from the theatre . . .

The unclaimed and those who died during birth
Lie somewhere rockier, with the disinterred,
And the parts of atheists no one could dissect,
Shovelled into an island with worse views, upriver.

This is the city's archipelago, its dead –
They watch new buildings going up in spring,
And wait in autumn for the reassertion of air,
For the middle distance to reappear,

Like space in the medina when trading is over
And the crowd disperses indoors to prayer.
There are bright skiffs of steam in the air holes,
And swallows planning their homeward journey.

❧

Forget the transplant your father waited for,
The middle-of-the-night phone call that never came.
Forget the parched brain fizzing with morphine,

The body turning away in the bed, bored.
Forget the negligence of nurses.

Start with a daughter looking for her father,
Waking in shuttered rooms, in vandalised suites.
Start with your father listening for his mother,
Waking in the Acton orphanage, in wet sheets.

Forget the children's sandpit after rain.
Forget the pitch contour of rain . . .
It flaps like leather soles on last year's slippers,
Muffles the sound of binmen lobbing rubbish.

Start anywhere, everything dissipates.
Wet brains batter the limousine at noon.
End as a girl again, even Isolde,
Stranded in front of the fallen curtain,
Starting to sing.
End with a happy birthday, last but one.

You started dying on the morning you were made
While your father soaped himself in the sink
And your mother worked a porcelain-handled knife
Into a Simnel cake, sucking a marzipan ball.
Crumbs flew like chaff behind the harvester.
The letters of the code flipped in their pairs,
AATCCGCT: the odd proliferated error.

Because this is what death is:
Grant me the patience.

❦

Start with a woman watching a man
Catching his daughter. End with a photo.
End as a woman older than either,
Feeling her own child sag in her arms,
Seeing it all, now for the first time,
After the ending:

The sideboard with the touched-up teak veneer,
Your mother's watchful shrug of hair,
And your own mouth slewed with laughter,
Feet tilted like a landing goose,
Falling, and your father's slender hands
Stretched out in the wind,
Henna-stained, praying.
Northolt, the old front room,
The photo with its reddish colour cast.
The faded figure in the catacomb,
Scouring the ceiling.

Watch contre-jour, a shadow
In the shade of the capiz-shell lamp,
A mother and the child you were.
You have been among the living twice,
And loved both times.
You have fallen in the lurid air.

Acknowledgements

'You, Very Young in New York' and 'Repeat until Time' first appeared in *Areté* magazine. 'The Sandpit after Rain' is in memory of my father, John O'Sullivan (1950–2014).

My friends have been generous with their encouragement for many years. I am especially grateful to those who scrutinised early drafts of these poems: Clare Pollard, Lara Feigel, Yael Goldstein Love, Sarah Howe, Amelia Klein, Roddy Lumsden, Patrick Mackie and Namwali Serpell. For careful attention to the final form, I would like to thank Matthew Hollis and Lavinia Singer at Faber, and typesetter Hamish Ironside. I am also indebted to my colleagues at New College, Oxford, for granting me leave from teaching, and to the Leverhulme Trust for support in the form of a Philip Leverhulme Prize. My mother and husband made it possible for me to finish the book during maternity leave, and I thank them with love.

For quotations, I gratefully acknowledge: Joan Didion, Theodor Adorno, Henry James, F. Scott Fitzgerald, Heraclitus, Philip Larkin, Hugh Kenner, William Shakespeare, Percy Bysshe Shelley, E. M. Forster, Horace, Claude Monet, James B. Conant, Robert J. Oppenheimer, Suetonius, Petronius, T. S. Eliot, and the anonymous authors of the *Li Ki* and the *Kalevala*.